It's Raining Laughter

❖ Poems by Nikki Grimes ❖

Photographs by Myles C. Pinkney

Boyds Mills Press

For Mr. and Mrs. James Buchanan, who blessed my young life with a dose of joy
—N. G.

Dedicated to God; and the children of this book; and to my parents, Jerry
and Gloria Jean Pinkney, who have helped me
—M. C. P.

Text copyright © 1997 by Nikki Grimes
Photographs copyright © 1997 by Myles C. Pinkney

The photographer would like to thank Greig Farm and Adriance
Memorial Library for use of their grounds and buildings.

Published by Wordsong
Boyds Mills Press, Inc.
A Highlights Company
815 Church Street
Honesdale, Pennsylvania 18431
Printed in China

Library of Congress Cataloging-in-Publication Data
Grimes, Nikki.
It's raining laughter / by Nikki Grimes;
photographs by Myles C. Pinkney.
p.   cm.
Summary: A collection of poems about children growing up, illustrated with
photographs of African American children.
Originally published by Dial Books for Young Readers, New York, 1997
ISBN 1-59078-077-9
1. Children—Juvenile poetry. 2. Growth—Juvenile poetry.
3. Afro-Americans—Juvenile poetry. 4. Children's poetry, American.
[1. Growth—Poetry. 2. Afro-Americans—Poetry. 3. American poetry.]
I. Pinkney, Myles C., ill. II. Title.
PS3557.R48998217 1997   811.54-dc20   96-9631   CIP   AC

Designed by Nancy R. Leo
First Boyds Mills Press paperback edition, 2005

Visit our Web site: www.boydsmillspress.com

10 9 8 7 6 5 4 3 2 1

It's Raining Laughter

I'm Jelayni. Patrice.
Tiana. Charnelle.
When I was born
my mama gave me names that sing
so anyone could tell
that even my newborn-baby cries
were music to her ears.

I am melody.
I've a symphony in me
bound by my fingers.
I'll practice now,
make a joyful noise 'til I learn how
to help those poor
crescendos and *fortissimos*
escape their pudgy prisons.

I'm a goofy giggler,
a sadness chaser,
a good-mood maker.
I find laughter in a cup,
pour it over all I see.
And when I smile, Grandma calls me
the spitting-image of God's joy.

I'm a hang glider,
a wild-wave rider,
a steep-cliff climber.
Someday there'll be
poems about me blazing new trails
just because I could.

I might be Joetta,
or Donelle Alshon,
named after Aunt Ellen
and Grandfather Don.
Whatever I'm called
or may grow up to be,
I'm a work of art now, obviously.

Where'd You Get Them Names?

We got wade-in-de-water names
(Where'd you get them names?)
Goin'-ova-Jordan names
(Lord must *love* them names.)

We got Zulu, Juju, Mojo names
(Where'd you get them names?)
Leopard, Lion-spirit names
(*Who* taught you them names?)

We got drenched-in-honey-butter names
(Where'd you get them names?)
Mississippi-showboat names
(Who give yawl them *names*?)

"Hush," says Daddy, "'bout them names."
(Where'd you find them names?)
"They're new names, old names,
Good names, proud names."

(Be *glad* you got them names!)

Remember

I remember that time
I stood on stage
at the Countee Cullen Library
and recited my poem
and hardly noticed
how loudly my knees
were knocking
'cause you were there
smiling from the front row
to let me know
that I was doing
just fine.

At the Library

I flip the pages of a book and slip inside,
where crystal seas await and pirates hide.
I find a paradise where birds can talk,
where children fly and trees prefer to walk.
Sometimes I end up on a city street.
I recognize the brownskin girl I meet.
She's skinny, but she's strong, and brave, and wise.
I smile because I *see me* in her eyes.

Running

When I run,
I don't have to think
about home or school.
There're no rules
to memorize,
or break, or keep.
I don't have to compete
or try to beat anybody
to prove a point.
All I have to do
is take a deep breath
and go.
I don't even
have to know
how fast
I fly.

Sideways Beauty

Mama says I'm wiry.
Aunt Mae says I'm a stick.
And one dumb kid at school
calls me a black toothpick.

I hate being skinny.
Good thing I got a rear.
That way when I turn sideways,
I don't disappear!

Four Eyes

I used to hate
my eyeglasses
'til Daddy told me
they were only
picture frames
protecting two
perfectly beautiful
works of art.

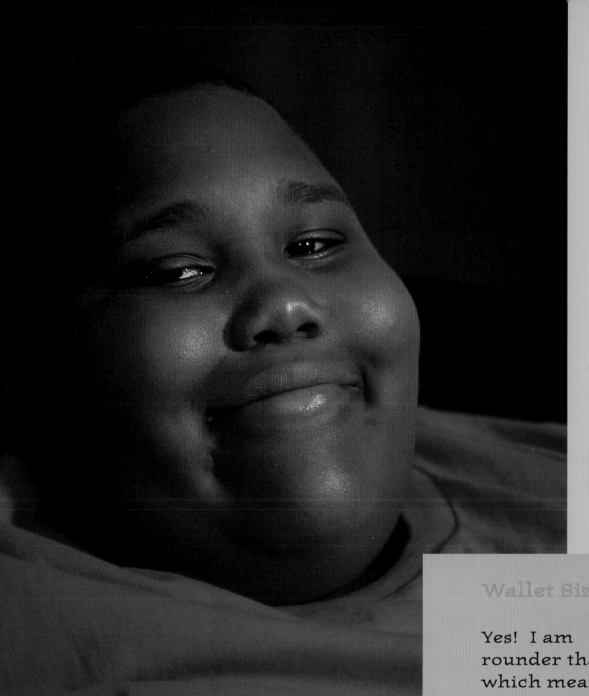

Wallet Size

Yes! I am
rounder than most
which means
there is more of me
to love.
If you're smart
you'll cherish
my portrait
and me, see
how snugly I fit
in the pocket
of your heart.

Listen

Listen:
Let me tell you
where things stand.
Each day is like fruit
resting ripe in my hand.
Will I sample its sweetness?
Will I toss it away?
Will I let you steal it?
I got one thing to say:
Don't try it.
Don't try it.

Friends Again

There was no *I* that day
but only *we*.
The stupid fight that drove
my friend from me
forgotten as we squinted
at the sun. . . .

And laughed for no good reason,
needing none.

The Laughing Bug

I caught the laughing bug
the other day.
Who spread the germ to me
it's hard to say.

My brother told
a yucky monster story,
and had to laugh himself
it was so gory.

My sister squealed
with joy, and giggled when
Dad tickled her. Did I
start laughing then?

Someone infected me
with glee that day.
I wonder if God's love
could spread that way.

I AM

I laugh
shout
sing
smile
whisper
hum
howl
gurgle
giggle
sigh.

I am
joy.